The World in My Neighborhood

Dona Herweck Rice

Many Parts, One Whole

Wherever you live, a mix of people live around you.

Each has their own story.

Each is part of the whole.

And the whole makes one beautiful world!

Jump into Fiction

In the Mix

Carlo was late.
He turned the corner and
wham!

He kicked two paint cans.

Mia was painting a mural. It showed how neighbors mix together like flowers in a garden.

Mia smiled at Carlo.
"Now you are in the mix too!"

Back to Nonfiction

The Sights

Look around.

This neighborhood is beautiful in many ways.

The buildings are old.

But old is not bad.

The buildings show the work of many skilled hands.

This makes them beautiful.

The Art of Buildings

Some people design buildings.

They are called *architects*.

They make buildings look good and stand strong.

210

Artwork is everywhere.
It is on walls and signs.
The people who make the art
come from all over the world.
Art is on people too!

Think and Talk

What art do you see in the picture?

Keep looking.
There are many people to see.
No two are the same.
Everyone has their own style.
They make the neighborhood beautiful too.

The Art of Clothes

Some people design clothes.
They are called *fashion designers*.
They design clothes to look good and fit well.

The Sounds

Now listen.

There are many sounds.

Each one is unique.

But together they make music.

It is the song of the neighborhood.

Sing along!

Music to My Ears

Music is made of notes.
Each note is a sound.
The notes are put together to make a melody.
The melody is the song.

The vendor calls to customers.
Motors roar, and horns blast.
People talk and laugh.
They are part of the music too.

Think and Talk

What sounds do you hear where you live?

The Smells

Smell that!
The scent of garlic drifts from the pizza place.
The smell of sizzling peppers comes from the taco cart.
They smell delicious!

On the Nose

People breathe in smells. The smells are in the air. Nerves inside the nose pick up the scents and tell the brain what the smell is.

The smells of gas and oil from passing cars fill the air.
Diesel fuel warns that a bus is near.
These smells are strong and powerful.
The mix of them can be beautiful too!

Not for Everyone

Not everyone has the same sense of smell. Some people find a smell nice while others do not.

A Beautiful Mix

A mix of sights, sounds, and smells fills the neighborhood.
They make it unique.
They belong to the people of the neighborhood.
This is their place.
And the mix is beautiful.

Better Together

"Better together" is an old saying. It means that people do better when they work together.

Civics in Action

We each add something special to our neighborhood. But some people may be scared to be different. You can help others feel proud. You can help them celebrate their differences.

1. Write a letter to a neighbor.
2. Tell them what you like about them.
3. Tell them why you are glad to be neighbors.